Summer Blast
Getting Ready for Second Grade

Reading   Math   Writing

Art

Puzzles   and more!

Author
Jodene Smith, M.A.

SHELL EDUCATION

Standards
To learn important shifts in today's standards, see the Parent Handbook on pages 121–126. For information on how this resource meets national and other state standards, scan the QR code or visit our website at http://www.shelleducation.com and following the on-screen directions.

Publishing Credits

Corinne Burton, M.A.Ed., *President*; Emily R. Smith, M.A.Ed., *Content Director*; Jennifer Wilson, *Senior Editor*; Robin Erickson, *Multimedia Designer*; Valerie Morales; *Assistant Editor*; Stephanie Bernard, *Assistant Editor*; Amber Goff, *Editorial Assistant*; Mindy Duits, *Cover Concept*

Image Credits

pp. 5–6, p. 12, p. 41, p. 76, p. 89, p. 92, p. 101: iStock; All other images Shutterstock

Standards

Shell Education
5301 Oceanus Drive
Huntington Beach, CA 92649-1030
http://www.shelleducation.com
ISBN 978-1-4258-1552-3
© 2016 Shell Educational Publishing, Inc.

Table of Contents

Introduction

Weekly Activities

Appendices

Welcome to Summer Blast!

Dear Family,

Welcome to *Summer Blast: Getting Ready for Second Grade.* Second grade will be an exciting and challenging year for your child. There will be plenty of new learning opportunities, including more complex books to read and more work with larger numbers! Interesting new topics in science and social studies will help keep your child engaged in the lessons at school.

Summer Blast was designed to help solidify the concepts your child learned in first grade and to help your child prepare for the year ahead. The activities are based on today's standards and provide practice with essential skills for the upcoming grade level. Keeping reading, writing, and mathematics skills sharp while your child is on break from school will help his or her second-grade year get off to a great start. This book will help you BLAST through summer learning loss!

Keep these tips in mind as you work with your child this summer:

- Set aside a specific time each day to work on the activities.

- Complete one or two pages each time your child works, rather than an entire week's worth of activity pages at one time.

- Keep all practice sessions with your child positive and constructive. If the mood becomes tense or you and your child get frustrated, set the book aside and find another time to practice.

- Help your child with instructions, if necessary. If your child is having difficulty understanding what to do, work through some of the problems together.

- Encourage your child to do his or her best work and compliment the effort that goes into learning.

Enjoy the time learning with your child during his or her vacation from school. Second grade will be here before you know it!

What Does Your Rising Second Grader Need to Know?

1. Use common vowel teams (*ea*, *ee*, and *ie*) for reading.

2. Read literary texts such as folktales, fairy tales, and classic myths.

3. Write various texts such as letters and book reports.

4. Add and subtract numbers up to 20.

5. Understand what place value is.

6. Know time and money and how they relate to the real world.

7. Understand the life cycles of plants and animals.

8. Know that materials come in different forms such as solids, liquids, and gases.

9. Understand time lines and important heroes.

10. Know why important buildings, statues, and monuments are associated with state and national history.

Things to Do as a Family

General Skills

◆ Make sure your child gets plenty of exercise. Children need about 60 minutes of physical activity each day. The summer months are the perfect time to go swimming, ride bicycles, or play outdoor team sports.

◆ Help your child become organized and responsible. Have places for your child to keep important things. Take time to set up a schedule together. Use a timer to keep track of time spent on different activities.

Reading Skills

◆ Set a reading time for the entire family at least once every other day. Help your child choose a book at a comfortable reading level. Take turns reading aloud one page at a time. Be sure to help him or her sound out and define unfamiliar words.

◆ After reading, be sure to talk to your child about what they've read. Encourage your child to share details from the books they read.

Writing Skills

◆ Set up a writing spot for your child. Have all of his or her writing materials in one special place. Having a designated area to write will help your child see writing as an important activity.

◆ Encourage your child to write emails, texts, or letters to friends and family members who live near and far.

Mathematics Skills

◆ Encourage your child to practice telling time. Give your child an allotted amount of time to do an activity they enjoy. Ask your child to use a clock to help figure out his or her playtime. For example: *What will the clock look like when your 15 minutes of video games are up?*

◆ Include your child in grocery shopping. Use the prices in the store to ask your child questions. For example: *Apples are 50 cents each. If you have two dollars, how many apples can you buy?*

Summer Reading Log

Directions: Keep track of your child's summer reading here!

Date	Title	Number of Pages

Top 5 Family Field Trips

A Trip to a Zoo

Bring a blank paper on a clipboard with you. Fold the paper into four even squares and label them *Desert*, *Ocean*, *Rainforest*, and *Forest*. Have your child guess which habitat each animal belongs in and write the name in the square. Then, have your child read the information placard and determine if your child guessed correctly.

A Trip to a Museum

Your first stop should be the gift shop. Have your child pick out five postcards of artifacts or paintings in the museum. Then, as you visit the museum, your child should be on the lookout for the five items he or she chose. It's an individual scavenger hunt! (Postcards usually have a bit of information about the pictured item to help you find it.) If he or she finds all five, you can celebrate the great accomplishment! Plus, your child gets to keep the postcards as memories of the day.

A Trip to a Library

Ask your child about a new skill he or she is interested in learning. Your child can then use the digital catalog to search for books on that skill that match his or her reading level. He or she can choose two books about the topic, check them out, and enjoy learning a new skill!

A Trip to a National Park

The National Park Service has a great program called Junior Rangers. Be sure you check in with the rangers at the visitors' center to see what tasks your child can complete to earn a Junior Ranger patch and/or certificate. Before you travel to the park, your child can also go to the WebRangers site (http://www.nps.gov/webrangers/) and check out your vacation spot, play games, and earn virtual rewards!

A Trip to a Farmers Market

Farmers markets are great places to learn about how different fruits and vegetables are grown. For each fruit or vegetable stand, have your child identify whether it is grown in the ground or on a bush or tree. Encourage your child to ask the seller/farmer about the steps it takes to grow the plant. Have your child pick out a fruit or vegetable he or she learned about to buy and enjoy with dinner that night!

Top 5 Family Science Labs

Science Fun for Everyone—Lava Lamp

http://www.sciencefun.org/kidszone/experiments/lava-lamp/

Learn about density in this fun and simple experiment.

Science Fun—Dancing Raisins

http://scifun.chem.wisc.edu/homeexpts/dancingraisins.htm

Learn about carbonated beverages and carbon dioxide while having fun!

Science Fun—Candy Chromatography

http://scifun.chem.wisc.edu/homeexpts/candy.htm

Learn about the dye used in the common candies you enjoy.

Science Bob—Roll a Can With Static Electricity

http://sciencebob.com/roll-a-can-with-static-electricity/

Learn about static electricity with this easy-to-follow experiment.

Science Bob—How to Make Slime

http://sciencebob.com/make-some-starch-slime-today/

Learn about solids and liquids as you make your own substance.

Top 5 Family-Friendly Apps and Websites

Apps

Kids Fruit Shots—Maths Addition by TharSoft Labs

This app includes fun interactive addition games and will help your child practice adding single- and two-digit numbers.

Chicktionary by Soap Creative

This fun word game challenges players to unscramble letters to find different words.

KenKen Classic by KenKen Puzzle

This clever twist on Sudoku requires kids to solve math problems and use logical thinking.

Websites

Coolmath-Games.com

http://www.coolmath-games.com

This site focuses on improving mathematics skills through fun games, puzzles, mazes, and exercises.

Funbrain

http://www.funbrain.com/kidscenter.html

Fun, arcade-style games covering a variety of concepts at all grade levels make this a great website for busy families.

Top 5 Games to Play in the Car

I'm Going on a Picnic Memory Game

Start off by saying, "I'm going on a picnic, and I'm bringing . . ." and follow it with an item that starts with the letter *A*, such as apples. The next player repeats what the first person says and adds on a *B* item. For example, "I'm going on a picnic, and I'm bringing apples and bananas." Continue until you complete the entire alphabet. The first person to forget one of the previous items is out. Feel free to adjust the leniency with younger players.

Create a Story

Create a story one sentence at a time. Start off by creating an opening sentence of a story. You might say, "Once upon a time, there was a small village of talking chickens." The next player must continue the story by adding on the next sentence.

I Spy (with a Twist)

This is a favorite car ride game. However, it can get boring when you play with just colors, so add a small twist. Instead of always spying colored objects, spy objects that are certain shapes, distances, or textures. You might say, "I spy an oval." Or, "I spy something about a mile away." Or even, "I spy something bumpy." It certainly makes the game more interesting. And, don't forget to allow yes/no critical thinking questions. For example, "Is the object high in the sky?" Or, "Is the object inside the car?"

Add It Up License Plates

Call out the numbers on a license plate and see who can add them up the fastest! For example, if the license plate number reads 1ABC234, players would add 1 + 2 + 3 + 4. The first person to answer correctly gets a point. The first person to reach 10 points wins! The total can be varied depending on the length of the car ride.

Who Am I?

Think of an important person in history. Give your child a clue about the person's identity by revealing a characteristic or an important date or event. For example, you could say, "I was president of the United States." Then, answer yes/no questions to give clues about the person's identity. Your child might ask, "Were you the first president of the United States?" Keep answering yes/no questions until the person's identity is guessed correctly.

Top 5 Books to Read Aloud

The Giving Tree by Shel Silverstein

This classic story follows the lifelong friendship between a boy and a tree. The underlying theme of generosity is shown through its simple drawings and emotional writing. This touching story offers beautiful examples of selfless love and undying friendship.

The Book With No Pictures by B.J. Novak

Simple yet imaginative, this humorous book is filled only with words in various fonts and bright colors. Perfect for reading aloud, each page prompts the reader to exclaim funny noises, silly words, and laughable sentences. The lightheartedness of this book will be sure to make your child giggle while introducing him or her to the idea that the written word can be fun and enjoyable.

Alexander and the Terrible, Horrible, No Good, Very Bad Day by Judith Voist

This book features Alexander, a young boy who is having one of the worst days of his life. Your child will enjoy this humorous contemporary classic while learning about managing family life and expressing emotions in a healthy and positive way.

Looking at Lincoln by Maira Kalman

This book blends history into a wonderful fiction story. The story follows a girl to the library as she learns more about Abraham Lincoln's incredible life. The colorful, vivid illustrations will captivate your child while the interesting content brings the history and facts of Lincoln's life to light in a fresh and exciting way.

Rosie Revere, Engineer by Andrea Beatty

Written in rhyming verse, this story of a shy girl who loves to invent gadgets and gizmos is perfect for reading aloud. Through the story, Rosie learns that you only truly fail when you stop trying. The lively and detailed illustrations bring Rosie's lesson of perseverance and determination to life.

Week 1

This week, blast through summer learning loss by:

◆ using past tense verbs

◆ answering questions about bodies of water

◆ writing a narrative

◆ creating a postcard about space

◆ solving a hundreds chart puzzle

◆ making fractions with pizza slices

◆ using pictures to solve a problem

◆ decoding symbols to identify biomes

◆ solving addition and subtraction equations

Words in Action

Directions: Rewrite each sentence to show past tense.
Hint: The underlined words need to be changed.

1. Jack <u>will go</u> to the farm.

    Jack went to the farm.

2. Jack <u>packs</u> a bag.

    _____

3. Jack <u>will ride</u> a pony.

    _____

4. He <u>sees</u> a cow.

    _____

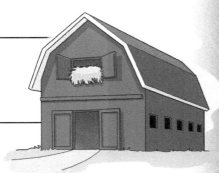

5. He <u>has</u> a lot of fun.

    _____

Directions: Write your own sentence with a past tense verb. Circle the verb.

_____

_____

So Much Water

Directions: Read the text. Then, answer the questions.

There are many different bodies of water. A bay is surrounded on three sides by land. A lake is made of fresh water. It is surrounded by land. A river starts at a mountain or glacier. It moves from high to lower ground. The lowest part of the river may spread out into a delta. It may also pour into an ocean. An ocean is a large body of saltwater that moves between sides of land called coasts. A stream is smaller than a river.

❶ Which of the following best describes an ocean?

Ⓐ moving water that starts on high ground

Ⓑ a large body of saltwater

Ⓒ a flat area of land at the mouth of a river

Ⓓ a large body of water with land on three sides

❷ What is the main topic of the paragraph?

Ⓐ There is a lot of water to drink.

Ⓑ There are many different bodies of water.

Ⓒ Land helps water.

Ⓓ A river starts at a mountain.

Hmmm, That Tasted Different . . .

Directions: Write about a time when something tasted different than you expected. Include details about the food item, such as describing what it looked like and how it tasted.

_____

_____

_____

_____

_____

_____

Draw a picture that goes with your writing.

Postcard from the Moon

Directions: Imagine you blasted off in a rocket and landed on the moon. Design a postcard that you could send back to Earth showing what you see there.

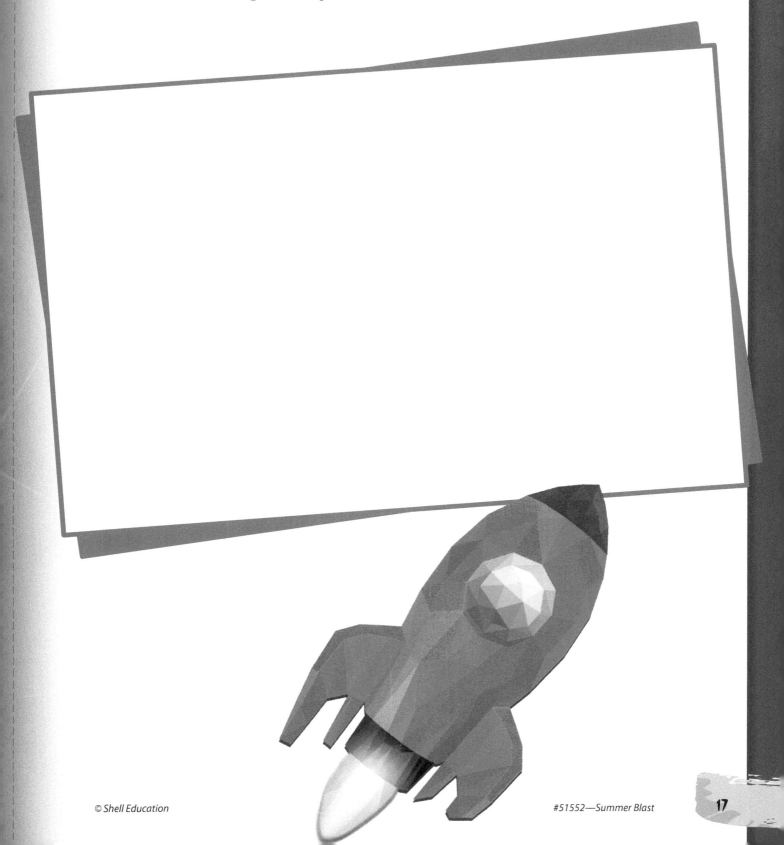

In a Muddle!

Directions: These pieces have been taken out of a hundreds chart. Write the missing numbers.

1

	2		
12	13		
	23		

2

		30
	39	
48		50
		60

3

33		35		
	44		46	47
			56	

4

58	
68	69
	80
	89
	100

Let's Share

Directions: Answer each question.

Amy shares a pizza with her friend.

❶ Divide the pizza in half.

❷ How many equal parts are there?

_____

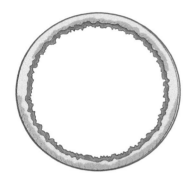

Amy shares another pizza that is the same size. She shares it with her sister, mom, and dad.

❸ Divide the pizza into fourths.

❹ How many equal parts are there?

_____

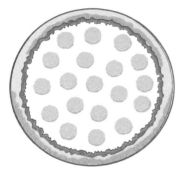

❺ Shade in the bubble for which pizza slices are bigger.

Ⓐ halves

Ⓑ fourths

Picnic Time!

Directions: Draw pictures on the plates to solve the problem below.

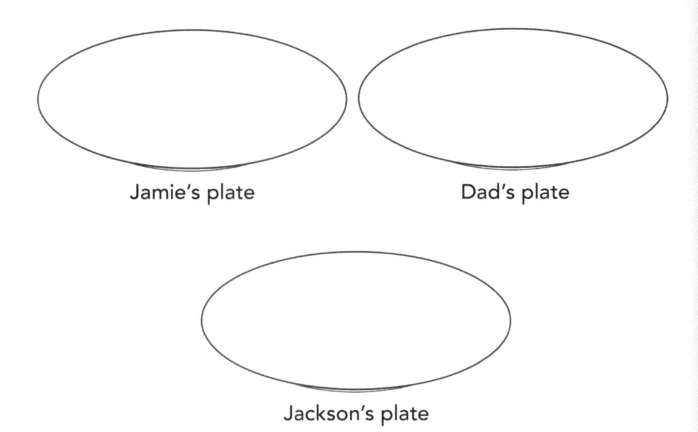

Jamie's plate

Dad's plate

Jackson's plate

Jamie and Jackson went on a picnic with Dad. Dad put 2 hot dogs on Jamie's plate and 2 hot dogs on Jackson's plate. He put 1 hot dog on his own plate. Draw the hot dogs. How many hot dogs are on the 3 plates?

_____ hot dogs

Biomes

Directions: Use the Code Bank to uncover the names of different biomes.

Code Bank

a	b	c	d	e	f	g	h	i	j	k	l	m
*	?	@	#	$	%	^	&	+	=	~	!	>
n	o	p	q	r	s	t	u	v	w	x	y	z
¢	©	÷	¬	Δ	π	∞	Ω	|	Σ	||	±	∧

1

—— —— —— —— —— ——
$ π $ Δ   ∞

2

—— —— —— —— —— ——
%   ©   Δ $ π   ∞

3

—— —— —— —— ——
©   @ $ *   ¢

4

—— —— —— ——
÷   ©   ¢   #

5

—— —— —— —— —— ——
∞   Ω   ¢   #   Δ   *

Math Boggle

28	59	16
72	43	87
35	60	91

Directions: Choose two numbers from the chart above. Write and solve two addition equations.

❶

❷

Directions: Choose two numbers from the chart above. Write and solve two subtraction equations. Remember the greater number must be first.

❸

❹

Challenge: Write an equation in which you add first and then subtract. **Hint:** You will need to choose three numbers.

Week 2

This week, blast through summer learning loss by:

- capitalizing proper nouns
- reading a folktale
- writing about your favorite game
- designing an amusement park
- adding rows of keys
- ordering blocks by size
- using time to solve a problem
- critically thinking about wants and needs
- acting out the motions of pushing and pulling

Find the Right Noun

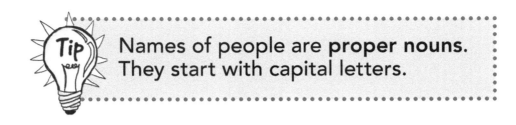

Tip Names of people are **proper nouns**. They start with capital letters.

Directions: Choose the correct noun from each pair.

1 _____*Ben*_____ went to the park with his ____*brother*____ .
     (Ben   ben)   (Brother   brother)

2 _____ told him to wear a _____.
     (Mom   mom)   (Hat   hat)

3 Please tell _____ that we are going.
     (Dad   dad)

4 I will take my _____, too.
     (Dog   dog)

5 I love taking _____ to the park.
     (Duke   duke)

Why Turtles Live in the Water

Directions: Read the text. Then, answer the questions.

Long ago, turtles lived only on land. Until one day, a group of hunters caught a turtle. They wanted to eat him, but they did not know how to get him out of his shell. They tried using a stick to get him out.

This was no ordinary turtle. This was a very clever turtle. He told the hunters, "Throw me into the water. Drown me. That will make it easy to get me out of my shell."

"That is a very clever idea," the hunters said. They threw the turtle into the water and began to dream of turtle soup.

But they lost their appetite when they saw the turtle swimming away! Far, far out to sea, he swam. As he escaped, the turtle said, "This is the life for me—a life at sea."

❶ What does this folktale explain?

- Ⓐ why turtles have shells
- Ⓑ why turtles' shells don't come off
- Ⓒ why turtles live in the water
- Ⓓ why turtles swim

❷ What is the turtle's real reason for having the hunters throw him into the water?

- Ⓐ because he was hot
- Ⓑ so he'd come out of his shell more easily
- Ⓒ to drown him
- Ⓓ to get away

My Favorite Game

Directions: Think about your favorite game. Write simple directions on how to play it. Include details about the players and how to win.

_____

_____

_____

_____

_____

_____

Draw a picture that goes with your writing.

#51552—Summer Blast   © Shell Education

My Best Amusement Park Ever!

Directions: Design a map of the best amusement park in the world! Draw your symbols in the Map Key. Then, use them as you design the layout of your map.

Map Key

Add the Rows

Directions: Count the keys in each row. Then, find the total number of keys.

1

_____

\+

_____

_____

2

_____

\+

_____

3

_____

_____

\+

_____

_____

4

_____

_____

\+

_____

_____

5

_____

_____

\+

_____

_____

6

_____

\+

_____

_____

#51552—Summer Blast

Let's Build

Directions: Use the shapes to answer the questions. Circle the correct answers.

A

B

C

1 Which block is shorter?   B   C

2 Which block is shorter?   A   B

3 Which block is the longest?   B   C   A

4 Order the blocks from shortest to longest. Write the letter of the block.

Shortest ⟶ **Longest**

5 Explain how you ordered the blocks.

_____

_____

_____

Time for Art

Mrs. Larson drew a clock on the board to show when art class starts. Karen says that art class starts at 11:30. Max says that art class starts at 10:30. Who is correct?

What Facts Do You Know?

How Can You Solve?

Who Is Correct?

Explain How You Know

Wants and Needs Sudoku

Directions: Read about wants and needs. Then, complete the steps below.

Needs are things you must have to live. **Wants** are things that are nice to have, but you do not need them to live.

Examples of Needs	Examples of Wants
food home clothes water	fancy shoes skateboard games television

Steps

Every mini grid must have *food*, *home*, *clothes*, and *water*.

Every row must have *food*, *home*, *clothes*, and *water*.

Every column must have *food*, *home*, *clothes*, and *water*.

food			clothes
	clothes	home	
	water		
home	food		water

Ready, Set, Action!

Directions: Read the definition. Act out some activities using different forces. Then, fill in the chart with actions that use push or pull.

force: energy that moves something

push: to move something away from you

pull: to move something toward you

Push	**Pull**

Week 3

This week, blast through summer learning loss by:

- ◆ replacing nouns with pronouns
- ◆ answering questions about the water cycle
- ◆ writing a persuasive letter
- ◆ drawing an animal out of your hand
- ◆ skip counting backwards
- ◆ answering questions about a bar graph
- ◆ using food items to figure out fractions
- ◆ using clues to create a chart
- ◆ identifying American heroes

Pronouns at Work

Directions: Rewrite the sentences to include pronouns from the Word Bank that replace the nouns.

Word Bank

he   He   him   She   ~~They~~

1. Mom and Jose went to the mall.

   They went to the mall.

2. Mom got a new puppy.

   _____

3. Jose wanted to buy games.

   _____

4. He waved at Sam.

   _____

Directions: Write a sentence. Include a pronoun. Circle the pronoun.

_____

_____

Drip, Drop, Down

Directions: Read the text. Then, answer the questions.

The water on Earth has existed for billions of years. But it hasn't always been in the same place.

Imagine a single drop of water. It may be floating in the ocean. Or, it could be in a small puddle.

As the sun shines, the water gets warm. When it gets warm enough, the droplet evaporates. It becomes water vapor. As a gas, it rises into the sky. There, it is very cold. The water vapor joins other cold droplets. Together, they form a cloud.

Droplets in the cloud grow heavy and wet. When they are too heavy to stay in the air, they fall. *Drip. Drop. Down.* Rain and snow fall upon the ground.

The water droplet returns to Earth. Slowly, it will trickle down to a lake. Or it may land in a river. In time, it will arrive at the ocean. And the cycle will begin again.

1 Which of the following does not give the reader a mental image?

- Ⓐ Imagine a single drop of water.
- Ⓑ Droplets in the cloud grow heavy and wet.
- Ⓒ Slowly, it will trickle down to a lake.
- Ⓓ The water on Earth has existed for billions of years.

2 What happens to water when it gets too warm?

- Ⓐ It falls back to Earth.
- Ⓑ It goes into the ocean.
- Ⓒ It evaporates and rises into the sky.
- Ⓓ The cycle begins again.

Dear Chef

Directions: Draw a picture of your favorite food on the plate. Write a letter to a chef convincing him or her to make your favorite food tonight for dinner.

Dear Chef,

_____

_____

_____

_____

_____

_____

_____

_____

Love,

_____

Hand Animal

Directions: Trace your hand in the space below. Then, draw a real or an imaginary animal using the outline of your hand. Color your picture.

Skip Backwards

Directions: Solve the problems. Use the number line to help you.

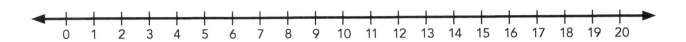

0 1 2 3 4 5 6 7 8 9 10 11 12 13 14 15 16 17 18 19 20

1 10 − 4 = ___6___

2 5 − 4 = _____

3 15 − 4 = _____

4 20 − 4 = _____

5 4 − 4 = _____

6 13 − 4 = _____

7 6 − 4 = _____

8 12 − 4 = _____

9 11 − 4 = _____

10 14 − 4 = _____

11 18 − 4 = _____

12 16 − 4 = _____

#51552—Summer Blast

Breakfast Graph

Directions: Use the bar graph to answer the questions.

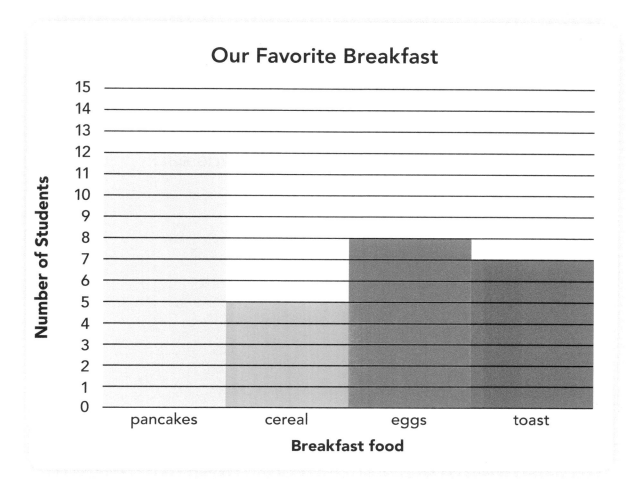

1 How many students choose cereal or eggs? _____

2 How many more students like pancakes than cereal?

_____

3 What is the breakfast that most students pick?

_____

What Fraction?

Directions: Read each problem. Draw a picture and write a fraction to show the answer.

1 Mrs. Webber cut a pizza into four equal slices. She ate one slices. What fraction of the pizza did she eat?

2 Amanda and Sarah share an apple equally. What fraction of the apple does Amanda eat?

3 Miles, Steven, and Tim share a pizza equally. What fraction of the pizza does Tim eat?

4 Sarah shared half of her banana with Miguel. What fraction of the banana did Miguel get?

Favorite Season

Directions: Use the clues to figure out each child's favorite season. Put a "+" in the chart below once you have figured out each child's favorite season.

Clues
Two of the children like seasons that begin with the same letters as their names.
Samir does not like a season that is too hot.
Zymal does not like to rake leaves.
Tim does not like snow.
Sophia enjoys warm weather.

	Fall	Winter	Spring	Summer
Sofia				
Zymal				
Tim				
Samir				

American Heroes

Number of Players

2

Materials

◆ *Heroes Cards* (pages 103 and 105)

Directions

1 Cut apart the *Heroes Cards* on pages 103 and 105.

2 Turn the cards facedown and mix them up.

3 Place the cards evenly into 4 rows.

American Heroes	American Heroes	American Heroes	American Heroes
American Heroes	She refused to give up her seat on a bus because she was black.	American Heroes	American Heroes
American Heroes	American Heroes	Rosa Parks	American Heroes

4 One player turns over two cards. If an American hero matches his or her accomplishment, keep the card pair. If the cards do not match, turn the cards back over. **Hint:** Remember where they are so you can make a match next time.

5 Take turns flipping over pairs of cards until all the American heroes have been matched to their accomplishments.

Week 4

This week, blast through summer learning loss by:

- combining sentences
- responding to a story about a ninja
- writing a sequel to a story
- drawing a vacation spot
- comparing numbers
- identifying shapes
- finding lengths
- unscrambling words about the Statue of Liberty
- measuring toys

Combining Sentences

Directions: Combine the sentences using the conjunctions **and** or **or**.

Tip **Conjunctions** can help combine two sentences.

1. Mom got us new clothes. Dad got us new clothes.

   Mom and Dad got us new clothes.

2. I had carrots for dinner. I had chicken for dinner.

   _____

   _____

3. I don't have a pencil. I don't have a pen.

   _____

   _____

4. Can I borrow your pencil? Can I borrow your pen?

   _____

   _____

The Ninja's Surprise

Directions: Read the text. Then, answer the questions.

The ninja hid in the shadow of a tree. He waited until a cloud passed in front of the moon. Swiftly, he darted up the castle wall until he found his target.

He eyed the sleeping princess. This was going to be easier than he had thought. The princess rolled over. He saw the ring. Focused on his mission, he crept forward and closed his hand around her finger.

Suddenly, the princess leapt from the bed. Her foot made contact with his leg. She grabbed his arm and flipped him onto the floor.

"The ring is mine!" she screamed.

Shocked, the ninja threw a firecracker across the room and darted through the window.

1. Why does the ninja close his hand around the princess's finger?

    Ⓐ because he is mad at her

    Ⓑ to get a ring

    Ⓒ because he likes her

    Ⓓ to keep her from getting away

2. Why does the princess flip the ninja?

    Ⓐ The ninja wakes her.

    Ⓑ She is showing off.

    Ⓒ She is protecting the ring.

    Ⓓ She is having a bad dream.

Another Ninja's Surprise

Directions: Write a sequel for *The Ninja's Surprise* on page 45. Describe what you think will happen when the ninja returns for the ring.

_____

_____

_____

_____

_____

_____

Draw a picture that goes with your writing.

Where Would You Go?

Directions: Where would you like to go on vacation—the mountains, the desert, the ocean? Use the doodle below as the beginning of a drawing to show where you would love to go. Be sure to draw yourself in the picture.

Comparing Numbers

Directions: Count the blocks. Circle the larger numbers.

1

19

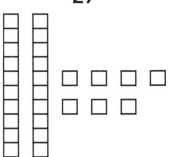

27

2

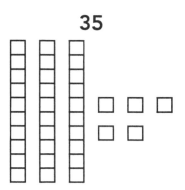

35

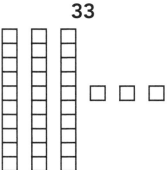

33

Directions: Draw a picture of each number. Then, compare. Write less than (<), greater than (>), or equal (=).

3 12 _____ 9

4 8 _____ 15

Shape Characteristics

Directions: Draw a shape to go in each box. There is more than one correct answer for some of the clues.

1. This shape has no curved sides.

2. This shape has all sides of equal lengths.

3. This shape has more than 5 corners.

4. This shape has 6 corners.

5. This shape has 5 corners and straight sides.

6. This shape has 4 sides but is not a square.

Scooter Sisters

Colleen and her sister each have a bike that is 3 feet long. They also each have a scooter that is 2 feet long. They keep their bikes and scooters in the garage along the wall. How long does the wall need to be to fit both bikes and both scooters?

What Facts Do You Know?

How Can You Solve?

How Long Does the Wall Need to Be?

Explain How You Know

#51552—Summer Blast

Lady Liberty

Directions: Unscramble the words to complete the sentences. Use the Word Bank to help you.

Word Bank

torch   copper   France

Harbor   pedestal   crown

1 The statue was a gift from _____.
(ceraFn)

2 It is in New York _____.
(Hobarr)

3 She is holding a _____.
(tcroh)

4 The statue stands on a _____.
(esdletap)

5 It is made out of _____.
(popcer)

6 There are seven points in the _____.
(wcnro)

Toy Measures

Number of Players

2

Materials

◆ *Direction Cards* (page 107)

◆ 3 toys or stuffed animals per player (The toys should vary in size.)

◆ ruler

Directions

1. Cut apart the *Direction Cards* on page 107. Turn them facedown in a pile.

2. Each player chooses 3 toys or stuffed animals.

3. One player chooses a card. Each player gets one point for each toy or stuffed animal that matches the description on the card. Keep track of the points on the score sheet below.

4. Play two more rounds.

5. Add the points from all three rounds to find the total number of points for each player.

6. Play again with new toys!

Names	Round 1	Round 2	Round 3	Total Points

Challenge: Make your own new cards to add to the pile.

Week 5

This week, blast through summer learning loss by:

- writing punctuation
- learning about new and old houses
- creating dialogue
- drawing sound waves
- adding numbers
- identifying times on analog and digital clocks
- solving word problems with subtraction
- finding words about space
- completing an experiment about pollen

Punctuation Station

Directions: Write a period, a question mark, or an exclamation point at the end of each sentence.

I love going to the zoo __!__

We go see the elephants first _____

They are huge _____

The giraffes are my favorite animals _____

What is your favorite animal _____

It was a great day _____

Directions: Write a sentence with correct punctuation.

_____

_____

Houses in History

Directions: Read the text. Then, answer the questions.

Then

Sod houses were built long ago in places where there were few trees. They were dug into a hill or out of the ground. These houses had dirt walls and floors. Roofs were made of grass and straw. Rain could leak through. Windows were made of oiled paper.

Now

Modern homes are often built with wood. They may have more than one door and many windows. Floors and walls are designed to keep the dirt out. Modern roofs are made of shingles or tiles. They keep it dry inside.

Which is the same between the houses? More than one answer may apply.

ⓐ They have roofs and windows.

ⓑ Windows are made of paper.

ⓒ Roofs are made of shingles.

ⓓ They have floors.

Drawing Dialogue

Directions: Look at the faces on the characters. Write what they are saying to each other in the speech bubbles.

Wave Art

Directions: Sound waves can be shown as lines. Draw lines to show how the sound waves below might look.

Examples

loud sound:

soft sound:

a cat meowing	
a siren	
someone whispering a secret	

Add Them Up!

Directions: Use the number line to solve the problems.

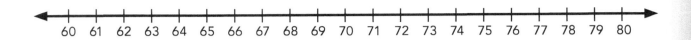

60 61 62 63 64 65 66 67 68 69 70 71 72 73 74 75 76 77 78 79 80

71 + 5	74 + 3	77 + 2

79 + 1	70 + 4	76 + 3

62 + 2	68 + 1	64 + 4

#51552—Summer Blast

What Time Is It?

Directions: Write the time. Use numbers and words.

Clock	Numbers	Words
6:30		
1:00		

Solve These

Directions: Draw a picture to match each problem. Write and solve the equation.

There were 6 fish in the lake. A man caught 2. How many fish are left?

_____ – _____ = _____ fish

Matt had 6 puppies. He gave 4 away. How many puppies are left?

_____ – _____ = _____ puppies

In Our Sky

Directions: Use the words from the Word Bank to fill in the blanks below. Then, find the words in the word search.

Word Bank

night	sun	revolves
Earth	moon	day

_____ is the planet we live on.

The closest star to Earth is the _____.

The _____ revolves around Earth.

The Earth's rotation causes _____ and _____.

The Earth _____ around the sun.

```
R   E   V   O   L   V   E   S

N   D   I   Y   R   U   A   H

D   T   V   P   O   G   R   Y

A   H   N   I   G   H   T   S

Y   S   E   A   S   N   H   U

N   U   O   D   M   O   O   N
```

Moving Pollen

Directions: Read the paragraph. Then, do the experiment.

Materials

- cheesy chips (with cheese powder)
- white paper

Parent Note

Review the ingredients in the cheesy chips to avoid any allergic reactions.

Flowers need pollen from other flowers to grow. Pollen gets to other flowers in many ways. Sometimes the wind blows it. Bees help move pollen, too. When a bee lands on a flower, pollen sticks to their bodies and legs. The bee then flies to another flower and some of the pollen from the first flower falls off into the second flower.

Experiment Steps

Eat some cheesy chips. Let the cheesy powder get all over your fingers as you eat them.

Touch a sheet of white paper with your fingers.

Talk about what you observe on the paper.

Talk about how that relates to a bee and pollen.

Week 6

This week, blast through summer learning loss by:

- describing nouns
- comparing stories
- writing about ice cream flavors
- designing currency
- comparing equations
- using data to create pictographs
- creating a word problem
- learning about phones today and long ago
- predicting the future

Describing Words

Directions: Write two nouns each adjective can describe.

1 rusty   *nail*   *fence*

2 sticky

3 fierce

4 slimy

5 sweet

6 brown

#51552—Summer Blast

Luci and the Three Dragons

Directions: Read the text. Then, answer the questions.

Once upon a time, there was a fierce dragon family. There was Papa Dragon, Mama Dragon, and Baby Dragon. One morning, they boiled a pot of nails for breakfast. But the nails were not rusty yet. So they went for a walk in the forest.

But the dragons did not know they were being watched. Luci, an alien with bright yellow tentacles, was circling above. She came from the planet Orb. And Orbians love to eat rusty nails. She landed and snuck into the cave.

Luci tasted the nails. "I like rustier nails," she said.

She sat on a chair. "I like stickier chairs," she said.

She rested on a bed. "I like slimier beds," she said.

Just then, the dragons returned. They saw Luci resting on the bed.

"Forget the nails!" Papa Dragon roared. "We will have an Orbian for breakfast!"

---

1 What is the same between this story and "Goldilocks and the Three Bears"? More than one answer may apply.

Ⓐ There are four characters.

Ⓑ There are chairs and beds in the story.

Ⓒ Someone gets eaten at the end of the story.

My Favorite Ice Cream

Directions: Label and color the ice cream with your favorite flavors. Then, write about them below.

Flavor 1: _____

Flavor 2: _____

Flavor 3: _____

_____

_____

_____

_____

_____

_____

New Currency

Directions: Artists help design our money. Design two new bills. You get to decide the bill values and the new looks!

Tricky True or False

Directions: Circle **true** if each problem is correct. Circle **false** if each problem is wrong.

1 $6 - 4 = 8 - 6$

$6 - 4 = 2$

$8 - 6 = 2$

(true) false

2 $5 - 1 = 8 - 4$

$5 - 1 = \underline{\hspace{2cm}}$

$8 - 4 = \underline{\hspace{2cm}}$

true   false

3 $2 - 2 = 3 - 2$

$2 - 2 = \underline{\hspace{2cm}}$

$3 - 2 = \underline{\hspace{2cm}}$

true   false

4 $2 - 1 = 9 - 8$

$2 - 1 = \underline{\hspace{2cm}}$

$9 - 8 = \underline{\hspace{2cm}}$

true   false

5 $7 - 4 = 5 - 3$

$7 - 4 = \underline{\hspace{2cm}}$

$5 - 3 = \underline{\hspace{2cm}}$

true   false

6 $5 - 5 = 8 - 7$

$5 - 5 = \underline{\hspace{2cm}}$

$8 - 7 = \underline{\hspace{2cm}}$

true   false

#51552—Summer Blast

Favorite Potato Chips

Directions: Use the information from the table to make a pictograph.

barbecue	sour cream and onion	salt and vinegar	plain
5	6	10	4

Favorite Potato Chips	
barbecue	
sour cream and onion	CHIPS CHIPS CHIPS CHIPS CHIPS CHIPS
salt and vinegar	
plain	

Directions: Answer the questions using the pictograph.

1 Which flavor is most popular? _____

2 How many more students like sour cream and onion than barbecue? _____

3 Which flavor is the least popular? _____

Line Drawings

Directions: Solve Problem A. Show your work. Then, write and solve your own problem about lines on shapes.

Problem A

Julietta drew a hexagon, a triangle, a rectangle, and two trapezoids. How many lines did Julietta draw in all?

Show your work:

Answer: _____

Problem B

_____

_____

_____

Show your work:

Answer: _____

Telephone Sudoku

Directions: Read about phones from today and from long ago. Then, complete the steps below.

Today, people talk on cell phones. There was a time when the phone was a new invention. Look at the photographs and names of the phones.

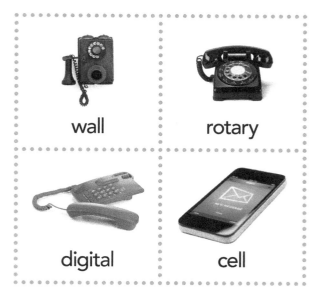

wall · rotary · digital · cell

Steps

Every mini grid must have *digital*, *wall*, *rotary*, and *cell*.

Every row must have *digital*, *wall*, *rotary*, and *cell*.

Every column must have *digital*, *wall*, *rotary*, and *cell*.

Note: The mini grid is where four boxes are together within the bolded lines.

	wall		digital
digital	rotary	cell	
wall			
		wall	cell

In the Future . . .

Number of Players
2–6

Materials

◆ *Item Cards*
(page 109)

◆ white paper

◆ crayons or
colored pencils

Directions

1 Cut apart the *Item Cards* on page 109. Place them facedown in a pile.

2 One person chooses a card. That person then draws a picture of what he or she thinks the card item will look like in the future.

3 Then, he or she shows the drawing to the others in the group and explains how it is different from now.

4 The next person adds to the picture, and then explains why he or she added to it.

5 Continue playing until all cards have been chosen.

Week 7

This week, blast through summer learning loss by:

- playing with root words
- comparing biomes
- writing about a wish
- creating a drawing of recycled materials
- identifying correct and incorrect equations
- using shapes to figure out fractions
- adding and subtracting with word problems
- learning about landforms
- racing with money

Working with Root Words

Directions: Divide the words below into prefixes and root words.

Word	Prefix	Root Word
1 misuse	mis	use
2 preheat		
3 restart		
4 unhappy		
5 untidy		
6 redo		

Comparing Biomes

Directions: Read the text. Then, answer the questions.

The desert is a special place. It is very dry. There is little rain there. Desert plants and animals can live without a lot of water. The cactus lives there. It stores water in its trunk. This helps it survive in the heat.

The desert is one type of biome. A biome is an area with certain plants and animals. The entire area has the same climate. These things make the area unique.

A rainforest is also a biome. It gets a lot of rain. It is also a very warm region. Large rainforests have animal and plant life. They can survive in damp and warm spaces. Various monkey species live in this biome.

Each biome is unique. People have to protect all biomes. Many living things depend on us. They want a healthy places to live.

❶ Which is true for all biomes?

   Ⓐ All biomes are wet.

   Ⓑ All biomes are cold.

   Ⓒ All biomes are unique.

   Ⓓ All biomes are full of people.

❷ What do people need to do for biomes?

   Ⓐ Protect them so that they are healthy areas.

   Ⓑ Measure the rainfall in rainforests.

   Ⓒ Stay away from hot and dry deserts.

   Ⓓ Locate animals in each biome.

Make a Wish

Directions: Imagine you pick a dandelion. You blow the seeds and make a wish. Describe what you wish for and why you are wishing for it.

_____

_____

_____

_____

_____

_____

_____

Trash Monster

Directions: Recycling is a great way to reduce trash. Draw a trash monster that is made out of recycled materials. For example, a coffee can could be the head. A box could be the body. Decide what you will use to make your monster.

True or False?

Directions: Is each equation true or false? If true, write it in the True oval. If false, copy it in the False oval.

Equations

1 + 6 = 7	2 = 9 − 6	10 − 8 = 18
12 = 12	8 + 1 = 11 − 2	8 = 7
4 = 7 + 3	4 = 6 + 2	4 + 5 = 1

True

False

Fraction Table

Directions: Complete the fraction table.

	How many equal parts does the shape have?	How many parts are shaded?	What is the fraction for the shaded parts?
1	2	1	$\frac{1}{2}$
2	4		
3		1	
4			$\frac{1}{4}$
5	3		

Add or Subtract?

Directions: Write each equation. Then, write the solution.

❶ Mia ate 6 crackers. Then, she ate 3 more. How many crackers did she eat?

❷ There are 5 toys on the floor. Two toys are put away. How many toys are on the floor now?

Equation: _____

Equation: _____

Solution: _____

Solution: _____

Directions: Write the words **forward** and **backward** to complete the sentences.

❸ Adding is like counting

❹ Subtracting is like counting

_____ .

_____ .

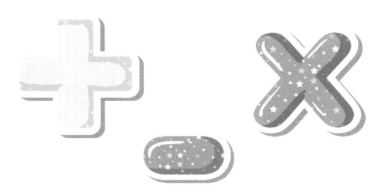

Earth Definitions

Directions: Read each definition. Then, write a word from the Word Bank on the lines.

Word Bank

mountain	glacier	island	valley
volcano	hill	cliff	canyon

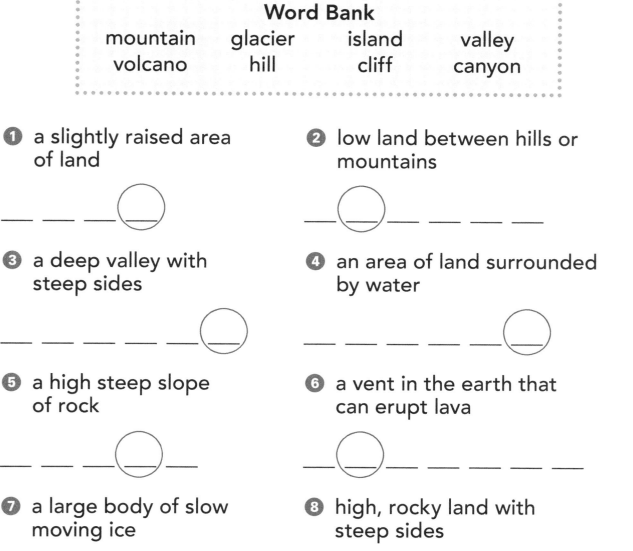

❶ a slightly raised area of land

— — — ◯ —

❷ low land between hills or mountains

— ◯ — — — —

❸ a deep valley with steep sides

— — — — — ◯

❹ an area of land surrounded by water

— — — — — ◯

❺ a high steep slope of rock

— — — ◯ —

❻ a vent in the earth that can erupt lava

— ◯ — — — — —

❼ a large body of slow moving ice

— — — — — — ◯ ◯ — — — — —

❽ high, rocky land with steep sides

Directions: Write the circled letter from each problem on the lines below to find the mystery word.

— — — — — — — — —

Race to a Dollar

Number of Players

2

Materials

◆ *Coin Value Cards* (page 111)

◆ coins in various denominations

◆ paper and pencil

Directions

1 Cut apart the *Coin Value Cards* on page 111 and turn them facedown in a pile.

2 One player turns over a card and uses coins to show the value on the card.

3 Write the value of the coins on a sheet of paper. Continue to add the value of coins on the cards each time it is your turn.

4 Take turns choosing cards, showing the values with coins, and adding the coin values together.
Note: Shuffle the cards again once all cards are flipped over.

5 The first person to get over one dollar wins.

Challenge: Race backwards from a dollar by subtracting.

Week 8

This week, blast through summer learning loss by:

- adding different endings to words
- reading a story about aliens
- writing a sequel
- designing a flag
- finding sums to equations
- measuring objects
- solving a word problem
- using directions to find a location
- making rain

Word Round Up

Directions: Add endings to each base word to make new words. Be careful—not all the endings will work with each base word.

> **Word Endings**
>
> -ed -s -ing -es

1. talk _talked, talks, talking_

2. stay _____

3. box _____

4. fish _____

5. start _____

Alien in the Basement

Directions: Read the text. Then, answer the questions.

Trevor heard a noise. It was coming from the basement.

"Stop, or I will eat you!" a voice hissed from below.

Trevor bravely moved down the stairs. "Who are you?" he asked.

"I'm an alien! My name is Zephtreme!" the alien replied.

Trevor ran back up the stairs to wait for his big brother.

When Trevor's brother stepped boldly onto the stairs, the alien said, "I have come to eat your guts!"

"You do not want to eat me!" said the brother. "I am too skinny. Eat my dad!"

Then, their dad went down the stairs.

The alien yelled, "I am evil, and I am hungry!"

"Well, I am DAD!" their father yelled as he ran toward the alien, scaring the alien away.

1 Which part of the story tells you why Trevor goes into the basement?

- Ⓐ Trevor hears a noise.
- Ⓑ Trevor runs back up the stairs.
- Ⓒ Trevor's brother steps onto the stairs.
- Ⓓ Their dad goes down the stairs.

2 How was the problem solved in the story?

- Ⓐ Trevor ran away from the alien.
- Ⓑ The alien ate Trevor's big brother.
- Ⓒ Their father scared the alien away.
- Ⓓ The characters locked the alien in the basement.

Alien in the Basement: Part 2

Directions: Think about the ending of *Alien in the Basement* on page 85. Write what you think will happen next.

_____

_____

_____

_____

_____

_____

Draw a picture that goes with your writing.

Design a Flag

Directions: The American flag has 13 stripes to represent the 13 original colonies. It also has 50 stars to represent the 50 states. Design a flag that represents you.

How does the flag represent you?

_____

_____

_____

_____

Find the Sums!

Directions: It is useful to memorize sums. Complete the charts. Then, try to memorize these. Ask an adult to quiz you.

1 + 1 = __2__   2 + 1 = _____   3 + 1 = _____

4 + 1 = _____   5 + 1 = _____   1 + 2 = _____

2 + 2 = _____   3 + 2 = _____   4 + 2 = _____

5 + 2 = _____   1 + 3 = _____   2 + 3 = _____

3 + 3 = _____   4 + 3 = _____   5 + 3 = _____

1 + 4 = _____   2 + 4 = _____   3 + 4 = _____

4 + 4 = _____   5 + 4 = _____   1 + 5 = _____

2 + 5 = _____   3 + 5 = _____   4 + 5 = _____

5 + 5 = _____   1 + 6 = _____   2 + 6 = _____

#51552—Summer Blast

More or Less?

Directions: Look around your house. Find each of the items shown below. Use a ruler to measure each one. Circle whether the item is less than a foot or more than a foot.

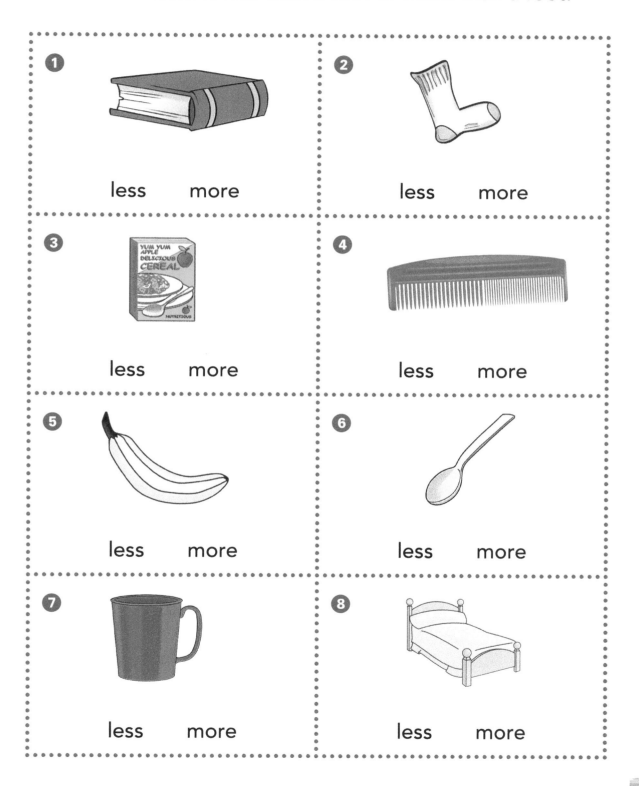

1. less   more

2. less   more

3. less   more

4. less   more

5. less   more

6. less   more

7. less   more

8. less   more

Apples for Sale!

Mr. Murphy sells red and green apples. Today, he sold 54 red apples and 45 green apples. Mr. Murphy wants to plant more of the apple trees that were most popular. Should he plant more red apple trees or green apple trees?

What Facts Do You Know?

How Can You Solve?

Which Apples Should He Plant More Of?

Explain How You Know

Where Are We Going?

Directions: Follow the directions to find out where you are going in the community.

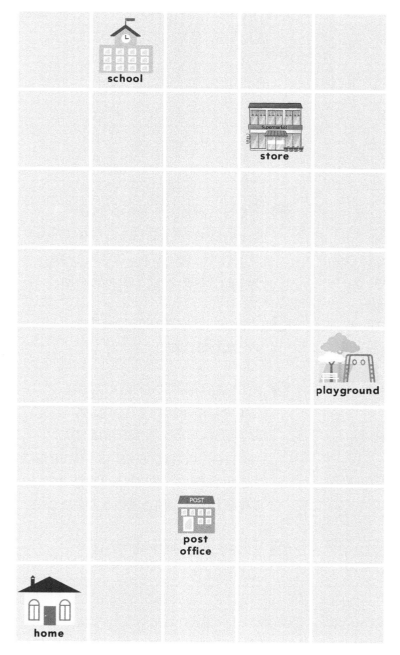

Directions

1 Start at home.

2 Go north 5 spaces.

3 Go east 2 spaces.

4 Go south 1 space.

5 Go east 1 space.

6 Go north 2 spaces.

I am going to the _____ .

Indoor Rain

Materials

- zip top baggie (sandwich or gallon size)
- water
- permanent marker
- tape

Directions

1. Lay the zip top baggie flat on a table. Draw waves across the bottom of the baggie. Draw a sun at the top of one corner and a cloud in the other corner of the bag.

2. Pour water into the baggie so that about an inch from the bottom. Seal the zip top well.

3. Tape the baggie to a window.

4. Observe the baggie throughout the day. When you see many water droplets gathered together at the top of the bag, tap the baggie.

5. Discuss what you observe.

#51552—Summer Blast

Week 9

This week, blast through summer learning loss by:

- reviewing language structure
- reading about city and country life
- writing about a vacation destination
- creating art with a leaf
- adding 10 more and 10 less to numbers
- organizing data
- calculating swimming laps
- using picture clues to identify animal babies
- declaring a law

Language Power

Directions: Read and answer each question.

① Circle the word that needs a capital letter.

Who has a birthday on july 15?

② Add a comma.

It is due on December 4 2016.

③ Write the correct pronoun.

Cindy loves _____ sister.
(their or her)

④ Unscramble the letters to make a word.

gvae _____

 #51552—Summer Blast

City and Country Living

Directions: Read the text. Then, answer the questions.

Life in the city is not like country living. *Urban* areas have more people. People live closer together in cities. There are more buildings. Big cities have more cars and roads. Some say that life moves faster in the city. There is always a lot going on. People are out at all times. It can be loud.

People in *rural* areas have space to move. They live close to nature. They may even grow plants or raise animals for a living. Life is quiet there. They do not hear the sounds of the city.

Sometimes, city dwellers like to visit the country. Country folks may like to spend time in the city, too. Most people are happy to go back home, wherever that may be.

1. Who are city dwellers?

   Ⓐ people who like cities

   Ⓑ people who live in cities

   Ⓒ people who hate cities

   Ⓓ people who travel to cities

2. Which place does the author claim is better?

   Ⓐ the city

   Ⓑ the country

   Ⓒ the suburbs

   Ⓓ Each place has good things to offer.

Beach or Mountains?

Directions: Would you prefer a vacation at the beach or in the mountains? Write about why you chose the place you did.

_____

_____

_____

_____

_____

_____

Draw a picture that goes with your writing.

Leaf Creation

Directions: Trace the outline of a leaf. Use the shape of the leaf to draw an animal. It can be real or imaginary.

Ten More and Less

Directions: Write the number that is 10 more and 10 less than each starting number.

	10 more	10 less
① 20	*30*	*10*
② 40		
③ 70		
④ 35		
⑤ 51		
⑥ 83		
⑦ 64		
⑧ 97		

Play Ball

Directions: Stacy asked 15 classmates about their hobbies. Organize the data in the chart below.

Allen	baseball	Frankie	swimming	Kevin	swimming
Bea	skiing	George	skiing	Laura	baseball
Cass	swimming	Helene	baseball	Mike	skiing
Derikka	baseball	Ivan	skiing	Naomi	swimming
Eddie	baseball	Justina	skiing	Oliver	baseball

1 Make one tally mark for each classmate's hobby. Write the total number for each hobby.

	Tally Marks	Total Number
baseball		
skiing		
swimming		

2 Write a question that can be answered using the tally chart. Give your question to a friend.

_____

_____

Swimming Laps

Josh swam 5 laps at the pool. Joe swam some laps, too. Together, they swam 16 laps. How many laps did Joe swim?

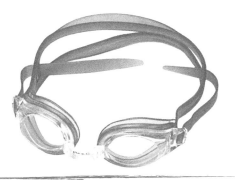

What Facts Do You Know?

How Can You Solve?

How Many Laps Did Joe Swim?

Explain How You Know

#51552—Summer Blast

Mothers and Babies

Directions: Use the letters and the picture clues to figure out the names of the animal babies.

Word Bank

eyas   pup   farrow

infant   fry   joey

Mother	Baby Hint	Baby Name
① fish	fr + Y	
② gorilla	+ f +	
③ kangaroo	jo + E	
④ bat	p +	
⑤ hog	f +	
⑥ hawk	+ as	

It's the Law

Directions: As a family, decide on a law you would like to have for the home. One person can write the law. Others can write the consequence for breaking the law.

Law

_____

_____

_____

_____

_____

Consequence

_____

_____

_____

_____

_____

 #51552—Summer Blast

Heroes Cards

Directions: Use these cards with the *American Heroes* game on page 42.

Abraham Lincoln	Martin Luther King Jr.
Susan B. Anthony	Theodore Roosevelt
Rosa Parks	Helen Keller

American Heroes

American Heroes

American Heroes

American Heroes

American Heroes

American Heroes

Heroes Cards (cont.)

Directions: Use these cards with the *American Heroes* game on page 42.

He was the 16th president. He led the United States in the Civil War.

He was the 26th president. He helped expand our nation's parks.

He fought for equal rights for all people.

She did not give up her seat on a bus because she was black.

She fought for women's rights.

She worked to help the blind and other causes.

American Heroes

American Heroes

American Heroes

American Heroes

American Heroes

American Heroes

Direction Cards

Directions: Use these cards with the *Toy Measures* game on page 52. Add your own descriptions on the blank cards.

tallest toy	shortest toy
taller than 4 inches	taller than 10 inches
shorter than 5 inches	shorter than 8 inches

Toy Measures

Toy Measures

Toy Measures

Toy Measures

Toy Measures

Toy Measures

Toy Measures

Toy Measures

Toy Measures

Toy Measures

Item Cards

Directions: Use these cards with the *In the Future . . .* game on page 72.

transportation	phones
clothing	toys
houses	schools

In the Future . . .   In the Future . . .

In the Future . . .   In the Future . . .

In the Future . . .   In the Future . . .

Coin Value Cards

Directions: Use these cards with the *Race to a Dollar* game on page 82.

30¢	5¢	20¢
10¢	35¢	15¢
25¢	50¢	25¢

Race to
a Dollar

Race to
a Dollar

Race to
a Dollar

Race to
a Dollar

Race to
a Dollar

Race to
a Dollar

Race to
a Dollar

Race to
a Dollar

Race to
a Dollar

Answer Key

Week 1

Words in Action (page 14)

1. Jack **went** to the farm.
2. Jack **packed** a bag.
3. Jack **rode** a pony.
4. He **saw** a cow.
5. He **had** a lot of fun.

So Much Water (page 15)

1. B
2. B

Hmmm, That Tasted Different . . . (page 16)

Check that the writing stays on topic and includes details about the food item.

Postcard from the Moon (page 17)

Check that the design includes details about what the moon looks like.

In a Muddle! (page 18)

1.

1	2	3	4
	12	13	
	22	23	

2.

		20
		30
38	39	40
48	49	50
		60
		70

3.

33	34	35	36	37
	44	45	46	47
	54	55	56	57

4.

58	59	
68	69	
78	79	80
	89	90
	99	100

Let's Share (page 19)

1.

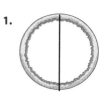

2. 2

3.

4. 4

5. A

Picnic Time! (page 20)

1. 5 hot dogs

Biomes (page 21)

1. desert
2. forest
3. ocean
4. pond
5. tundra

Math Boggle (page 22)

Check that the addition and subtraction of the numbers are correct.

Answer Key (cont.)

Week 2

Find the Right Noun (page 24)

1. **Ben** went to the park with his **brother**.
2. **Mom** told him to wear a **hat**.
3. Please tell **Dad** that we are going.
4. I will take my **dog**, too.
5. I love taking **Duke** to the park.

Why Turtles Live in the Water (page 25)

1. C
2. D

My Favorite Game (page 26)

Check that the writing includes clear directions on how to play the game.

My Best Amusement Park Ever! (page 27)

Check that the symbols in the map key are used on the map.

Add the Rows (page 28)

1. $4 + 4 = 8$
2. $3 + 3 = 6$
3. $5 + 5 + 5 = 15$
4. $4 + 4 + 4 = 12$
5. $3 + 3 + 3 = 9$
6. $5 + 5 = 10$

Let's Build (page 29)

1. C
2. A
3. B
4. C, A, B
5. The C block is shorter than the B and A blocks, so C is the shortest. Comparing the B and the A blocks determines the longest block, which is B.

Time for Art (page 30)

What Facts Do You Know?
Karen says 11:30. Max says 10:30. The clock's hour hand is after the 10 and before the 11, and the minute hand is on the 6.

How Can You Solve?
The hour hand is between the 10 and the 11. That means it is in the 10 o'clock hour. The minute hand points to the 6. That means 30 minutes. So, it is 10:30.

Who Is Correc?
Max is correct.

Explain How You Know
Because the hour hand is between the 10 and the 11, the hour is 10. Because the minute hand is pointing down to the 6, the minutes represented are 30. The time shown is 10:30.

Wants and Needs Sudoku (page 31)

food	home	water	clothes
water	clothes	home	food
clothes	water	food	home
home	food	clothes	water

Ready, Set, Action! (page 32)

Be sure that the players' actions represent pushing and pulling.

Week 3

Pronouns at Work (page 34)

1. **They** went to the mall.
2. **She** got a new coat.
3. **He** wanted to buy games.
4. He waved at **him**.

Check that the sentence includes a pronoun.

Drip, Drop, Down (page 35)

1. D
2. C

Answer Key (cont.)

Dear Chef (page 36)

Check that the writing contains reasons why the food should be made.

Hand Animal (page 37)

Check that the drawing has something to do with an animal.

Skip Backwards (page 38)

1. 6
2. 1
3. 11
4. 16
5. 0
6. 9
7. 2
8. 8
9. 7
10. 10
11. 14
12. 12

Breakfast Graph (page 39)

1. 13 students
2. 7 more students
3. pancakes

What Fraction? (page 40)

1. $\frac{1}{4}$
2. $\frac{1}{2}$
3. $\frac{1}{3}$
4. $\frac{1}{2}$

Favorite Season (page 41)

Sofia—Summer

Zymal—Winter

Tim—Fall

Samir—Spring

American Heroes (page 42)

Abraham Lincoln: He was the 16th president. He helped keep the country united through the Civil War.

Martin Luther King Jr.: He fought for equal rights for all people during the Civil Rights Movement.

Susan B. Anthony: She fought for the end of slavery and for women's rights.

Theodore Roosevelt: He was the 26th president. Construction on the Panama Canal began and expansion of the national parks happened under his leadership.

Rosa Parks: She refused to give up her seat on a bus because she was black.

Helen Keller: Deafened and blinded by a childhood disease, she overcame her disabilities and then worked for the blind and numerous other causes.

Week 4

Combining Sentences (page 44)

1. Mom and Dad got us new clothes.
2. I had carrots and chicken for dinner.
3. I don't have a pencil or a pen.
4. Can I borrow your pencil and pen?

The Ninja's Surprise (page 45)

1. B
2. C

Another Ninja's Surprise (page 46)

Check that the sequel is a continuation of the story on page 45.

Where Would You Go? (page 47)

Check that the drawing shows a location.

Answer Key (cont.)

Comparing Numbers (page 48)

1. 27
2. 35
3. 12 > 9; Check that 12 block counters are drawn on the left and 9 block counters are drawn on the right.
4. 8 < 15; Check that 8 block counters are drawn on the left and 15 block counters are drawn on the right.

Shape Characteristics (page 49)

1. Possible answers: triangle, rectangle, square, pentagon, hexagon, octagon, rhombus
2. Possible answers: any regular polygon
3. Possible answers: hexagon, octagon
4. hexagon
5. pentagon
6. Possible answers: rectangle, trapezoid, rhombus

Scooter Sisters (page 50)

What Facts Do You Know?
Colleen and her sister each have a bike that is 3 feet long. They each have a scooter that is 2 feet long. They keep their bikes and scooters in the garage along the wall.

How Can You Solve?
3 + 3 + 2 + 2 = 10 feet

How Long Does the Wall Need to Be?
The wall needs to be at least 10 feet.

Explain How You Know:
The bikes are 3 feet long. The scooters are 2 feet long. There are 2 bikes and 2 scooters. The garage needs to be 10 feet long.

Lady Liberty (page 51)

1. France
2. Harbor
3. torch
4. pedestal
5. copper
6. crown

Toy Measures (page 52)

Check that the toys are being measured correctly.

Week 5

Punctuation Station (page 54)

1. !
2. .
3. !
4. .
5. ?
6. !

Check that the sentence is written with correct punctuation.

Houses in History (page 55)

1. A and D

Drawing Dialogue (page 56)

Check that the dialogue shows the characters talking to one another.

Wave Art (page 57)

Check that the sound waves are tight and jagged for the louder sounds and wavier for the softer sounds.

Answer Key (cont.)

Add Them Up! (page 58)

1. 76
2. 77
3. 79
4. 80
5. 74
6. 79
7. 64
8. 69
9. 68

What Time Is It? (page 59)

1. 4:00; four o'clock
2. 6:30; six thirty
3. 10:30; ten thirty
4. 1:00; one o'clock
5. 12:00; twelve o'clock

Solve These (page 60)

1. 6 − 2 = 4 fish
2. 6 − 4 = 2 puppies

In Our Sky (page 61)

1. Earth
2. sun
3. moon
4. day; night
5. revolves

R	E	V	O	L	V	E	S
N	D	I	Y	R	U	A	H
D	T	V	P	O	G	R	Y
A	H	N	I	G	H	T	S
Y	S	E	A	S	N	H	U
N	U	O	D	M	O	O	N

Moving Pollen (page 62)

Make sure that the discussion relates to bees moving pollen.

Week 6

Describing Words (page 64)

Possible answers include:

1. rusty: nail, fence
2. sticky: webs, gum, glue
3. fierce: tiger, monster, warrior
4. slimy: mud, mold, snail
5. sweet: honey, candy, cake
6. brown: bear, chocolate, pine cone

Luci and the Three Dragons (page 65)

1. A and B

My Favorite Ice Cream (page 66)

Check that the writing reflects the flavors listed.

New Currency (page 67)

Check that the bills are designed and include values.

Tricky True and False (page 68)

1. true; 2 = 2
2. true; 4 = 4
3. false; 0 ≠ 1
4. true; 1 = 1
5. false; 3 ≠ 2
6. false; 0 ≠ 1

Answer Key (cont.)

Favorite Potato Chips (page 69)

Favorite Potato Chips	
barbecue	🛍️ 🛍️ 🛍️ 🛍️ 🛍️
sour cream and onion	🛍️ 🛍️ 🛍️ 🛍️ 🛍️ 🛍️
salt and vinegar	🛍️ 🛍️ 🛍️ 🛍️ 🛍️ 🛍️ 🛍️ 🛍️ 🛍️ 🛍️
plain	🛍️ 🛍️ 🛍️ 🛍️

1. salt and vinegar
2. one more student
3. plain

Line Drawings (page 70)

A: 21 lines

B: Check that the number of lines matches the number of lines in the drawings.

Telephone Sudoku (page 71)

cell	wall	rotary	digital
digital	rotary	cell	wall
wall	cell	digital	rotary
rotary	digital	wall	cell

In the Future . . . (page 72)

Check that the drawings reflect what the items might look like in the future and are not based on what the items look like now or what they looked like in the past.

Week 7

Working with Root Words (page 74)

1. misuse; mis, use
2. preheat; pre, heat
3. restart; re, start
4. unhappy; un, happy
5. untidy; un, tidy
6. redo; re, do

Comparing Biomes (page 75)

1. C
2. A

Make a Wish (page 76)

Check that the writing describes the wish and the reason for the wish.

Trash Monster (page 77)

Check that the drawing includes recycled materials.

True or False? (page 78)

True

$1 + 6 = 7$

$12 = 12$

$8 + 1 = 11 - 2$

False

$4 = 7 + 3$

$2 = 9 - 6$

$4 = 6 + 2$

$10 - 8 = 18$

$8 = 7$

$4 + 5 = 1$

Answer Key *(cont.)*

Fraction Table *(page 79)*

1. 1
2. $1, \frac{1}{4}$
3. $3, \frac{1}{3}$
4. 4, 1
5. $1, \frac{1}{3}$

Earth Definitions *(page 81)*

1. Equation: 6 + 3 = 9
   Solution: 9 crackers
2. Equation: 5 − 2 = 3
   Solution: 3 toys
3. forward
4. backward

Add or Subtract? *(page 80)*

1. hill
2. valley
3. canyon
4. island
5. cliff
6. volcano
7. glacier
8. mountain
   Mystery Word: landform

Race to a Dollar *(page 82)*

Check that the values of the coins match the values on the cards.

Week 8

Word Round Up *(page 84)*

1. talked, talks, talking
2. stayed, stays, staying
3. boxed, boxing, boxes
4. fished, fishing, fishes
5. started, starts, starting

Alien in the Basement *(page 85)*

1. A
2. C

Alien in the Basement: Part 2 *(page 86)*

Check that the writing contains the same characters as the story on page 85.

Design a Flag *(page 87)*

Check that the items on the flag reflect the artist.

Find the Sums *(page 88)*

1 + 1 = 2; 2 + 1 = 3; 3 + 1 = 4
4 + 1 = 5; 5 + 1 = 6; 1 + 2 = 3
2 + 2 = 4; 3 + 2 = 5; 4 + 2 = 6

5 + 2 = 7; 1 + 3 = 4; 2 + 3 = 5
3 + 3 = 6; 4 + 3 = 7; 5 + 3 = 8
1 + 4 = 5; 2 + 4 = 6; 3 + 4 = 7

4 + 4 = 8; 5 + 4 = 9; 1 + 5 = 6
2 + 5 = 7; 3 + 5 = 8; 4 + 5 = 9
5 + 5 = 10; 1 + 6 = 7; 2 + 6 = 8

More or Less? *(page 89)*

1. less
2. less
3. more
4. less
5. less
6. less
7. less
8. more

Apples for Sale! *(page 90)*

What Facts Do You Know?
54 red apples; 45 green apples

How Can You Solve?
54 red
45 green
54 > 45

Which Apples Should He Plant More Of?
He should plant more red apple trees.

Explain How You Know:
Mr. Murphy sold more red apples than green apples, so he should plant more red apple trees.

Answer Key *(cont.)*

Where Are We Going? (page 91)

I am going to the <u>store</u>.

Indoor Rain (page 92)

Discuss how the water droplets represent rain.

Week 9

Language Power (page 94)

1. Who has a birthday on **July** 15?
2. It is due on December **4**, 2016.
3. Cindy loves **her** sister.
4. gave

City and Country Living (page 95)

1. B
2. D

Beach or Mountains? (page 96)

Check that the writing includes reasons to support the beach or the mountains.

Leaf Creation (page 97)

Check that the drawing represents a real or imagined animal out of the leaf outline.

Ten More and Less (page 98)

1. 30; 10
2. 50; 30
3. 80; 60
4. 45; 25
5. 61; 41
6. 93; 73
7. 74; 54
8. 107; 87

Play Ball (page 99)

1. Baseball: ⅢⅡ I ; 6
   Skiing: ⅢⅡ ; 5
   Swimming: IIII ; 4
2. Check that the question can be answered by the chart.

Swimming Laps (page 100)

What Facts Do You Know?
Josh swam 5 laps; Josh and Joe swam 16 laps together.

How Can You Solve?
16 − 5 = 11

How Many Laps Did Joe Swim?
Joe swam 11 laps.

Explain How You Know:
Counting on from 5 to 16 or subtracting 5 from 16, you get 11.

Mothers and Babies (page 101)

1. fry
2. infant
3. joey
4. pup
5. farrow
6. eyas

It's the Law (page 102)

Check that the law makes sense and that the consequence is appropriate.

Parent Handbook

Dear Parents or Guardians,

Have you ever wondered why states have learning standards? Teachers used to determine what they would cover based on what content was included in their textbooks. That seems crazy! Why would educators put publishers in charge of determining what they should teach? Luckily, we've moved past that time period into one where educational professionals create standards. These standards direct teachers on what students should know and be able to do at each grade level. As a parent, it's your job to make sure you understand the standards! That way, you can help your child be ready for school.

The following pages are a quick guide to help you better understand both the standards and how they are being taught. There are also suggestions for ways you can help as you work with your child at home.

Here's to successful kids!

Sincerely,

The Shell Education Staff

College and Career Readiness Standards

Today's college and career readiness standards, including the Common Core State Standards and other national standards, have created more consistency among states in how they teach math and English language arts. In the past, state departments of education had their own standards for each grade level. The problem was, what was taught at a specific grade in one state may have been taught at a different grade in another state. This made it difficult when students moved from state to state.

Today, many states have adopted new standards. This means that for the first time, there is better consistency in what is being taught at each grade level across the states, with the ultimate goal of getting students ready to be successful in college and in their careers.

Standards Features

The overall goal for the standards is to better prepare students for life. Today's standards use several key features:

◆ They describe what students should know and be able to do at each grade level.

◆ They are rigorous.

◆ They require higher-level thinking.

◆ They are aimed at making sure students are prepared for college and/or their future careers.

◆ They require students to explain and justify answers.

Mathematical Standards

There are several ways that today's mathematics standards have shifted to improve upon previous standards. The following are some of the shifts that have been made.

Focus

Instead of covering a lot of topics lightly, today's standards focus on a few key areas at much deeper levels. Only focusing on a few concepts each year allows students more time to understand the grade-level concepts.

How Can You Help?	What Can You Say?
Provide paper or manipulatives (such as beans or pieces of cereal) as your child is working so that he or she can show his or her answer.	Is there another way you can show the answer?
Have your child explain his or her thinking or the way he or she got the answer.	What did you do to solve the problem? What were you thinking as you solved the problem?

Coherence

The standards covered for each grade are more closely connected to each other. In addition, each grade's standards are more closely connected to the previous grade and the following grade.

How Can You Help?	What Can You Say?
Help your child to make connections to other concepts he or she has learned.	What else have you learned that could help you understand this concept?
Ask your child to circle words that may help him or her make connections to previously learned concepts.	What words in the directions (or in the word problem) help you know how to solve the problem?

Fluency

The standards drive students to perform mathematical computations with speed and accuracy. This is done through memorization and repetition. Students need to know the most efficient way to solve problems, too!

How Can You Help?	What Can You Say?
Help your child identify patterns that will work for increasing speed and accuracy.	What numbers do you know that can help you solve this problem?
Encourage the most efficient way to solve problems.	Can you get the same answer in a different way? Is there an easier way to solve the problem?

Mathematical Standards *(cont.)*

Deep Understanding

Students must develop a very good understanding of mathematical concepts. A deep understanding of mathematical concepts ensures that students know the *how* and the *why* behind what they are doing.

How Can You Help?	What Can You Say?
Encourage your child to make a model of the answer.	How do you know your answer is correct? Can you show your answer in a different way?
Have your child explain the steps he or she uses to solve problems.	Can you teach me to solve the problem?

Application

Today's standards call for more rigor. Students need to have strong conceptual understandings, be able to use math fluently, and apply the right math skills in different situations.

How Can You Help?	What Can You Say?
Encourage your child to use multiple methods for solving and showing his or her answers.	Can you explain your answer in a different way?
Have your child circle words or numbers that provide information on how to solve the problem.	What words gave you clues about how to solve this problem?

Dual Intensity

Students need to develop good understandings of mathematical concepts and then practice those concepts.

How Can You Help?	What Can You Say?
Provide practice with concepts or basic facts your child is having trouble with.	What did you have difficulty with? How can you practice that?
Have your child identify where his or her breakdown in understanding is when solving a problem.	Where can you find the help you need?

Language Arts Standards

The following charts describe the key shifts in language arts standards and some great ways that you can help your child achieve with them.

Balancing Informational and Literary Texts

Students should read and have books read aloud to them that represent a variety of texts and have a balance of informational and literary texts.

How Can You Help?	What Can You Say?
Find topics your child is interested in and then find both fiction and nonfiction books on the topic.	Since you like dinosaurs, let's find a story about dinosaurs and an informational book that tells facts about dinosaurs!
Encourage your child to know features of informational and literary texts.	How do you know this book is informational? What features does this literary book have?

Knowledge in the Disciplines

Once students reach sixth grade, they are expected to gain information directly through content-area texts rather than have the information told to them. Younger students can read nonfiction texts to prepare for this transition in the middle grades.

How Can You Help?	What Can You Say?
Talk about science and social studies topics with your child in everyday conversations so that your child learns about related words and concepts.	I heard on the news that there will be a lunar eclipse tonight. Let's watch it together so that we can see the shadow of Earth come between the moon and the sun.
Provide a variety of experiences for your child so that he or she can use them when reading about a topic. It makes the topic easier to understand.	Let's go have fun exploring the tide pools! What do you think we will see there? (*ask before*) What did you see at the tide pools? (*ask after*)

Staircase of Complexity

Students should read grade-appropriate complex texts. They may not understand the content right away, but with support and time, they will eventually comprehend what they're reading.

How Can You Help?	What Can You Say?
Know your child's reading level. Help your child find books that are at the high end of your child's reading level.	I found these three books for you to read. Which one interests you?
Read books to your child that are above his or her reading level. It exposes him or her to more complex vocabulary, sentences, and ideas.	Which book would you like me to read to you?

Language Arts Standards *(cont.)*

Text-Based Answers

Students should be able to answer questions and defend their positions using evidence from texts. This evidence can include illustrations and other graphics.

How Can You Help?	What Can You Say?
Ask your child to explain his or her answer using evidence from a book.	How do you know that? How else do you know _____?
Ask your child to look for evidence about something you notice in a book.	What evidence is there that _____?

Writing from Sources

Students should easily reference the texts they are reading as they write about them.

How Can You Help?	What Can You Say?
Have your child underline in the text the answers to questions he or she is answering through writing.	Where is the evidence in the text? How can you include that in your written response?
Provide sentence frames to help your child reference the text.	On page _____, the author says _____.

Academic Vocabulary

Academic vocabulary is a student's ability to recognize, understand, and use more sophisticated words in both reading and writing. Having a strong vocabulary allows students to access more complex texts.

How Can You Help?	What Can You Say?
Model using precise vocabulary.	I noticed you used the word _____. Could you have used a stronger word?
Provide a wide variety of experiences for your child to learn new words. These experiences don't have to cost money. They can be simple, everyday activities!	We are going to get the oil changed in the car. I want you to see if you can find the mechanic in his overalls.

Doodle